TRAVEL GUIDE TO GIBRALTAR 2025

Explore the Best of History, Culture, and Adventure on the Rock

Nielsen Frye

© Nielsen Frye 2024 All rights reserved. This publication may not be reproduced, stored or transmitted in any form (electronic, mechanical, photocopying or otherwise) without the express written permission of the copyright owner.

Table of Contents

INTRODUCTION 6
CHAPTER 1: Getting to Gibraltar 8
    Flights and Airports 8
    Ferry Connections 10
    Border Crossings from Spain 12
CHAPTER 2: Getting Around 14
    Public Transportation 14
    How to Use the Bus System 14
    Car Rentals 15
    Walking and Cycling 18
CHAPTER 3: History and Culture 20
    Historical Overview of Gibraltar 20
    Cultural Heritage and Traditions 23
    Festivals and Events 26
    Cultural Etiquette 29
    Local Language and Phrases 31
HOW TO USE THE QR CODE 34
CHAPTER 4: Top Attractions 35
CHAPTER 5: Hidden Gems and Off-the-Beaten-Path 43
CHAPTER 6: Outdoor Activities 51
    Hiking Trails 59
    Scuba Diving and Snorkeling 62
    Kayaking and Paddleboarding 65

CHAPTER 7: Accommodation 68
    Luxury Hotels 68
    Boutique Hotels 69
    Budget-Friendly Options 70
    Family-Friendly Stays 71
    Romantic Getaways 73

CHAPTER 8: Dining and Cuisine 75
    Must-Try Dishes 75
    Traditional Tavernas 77
    Fine Dining Restaurants 78
    Cafes and Bakeries 79
    Local Markets and Food Tours 82

CHAPTER 9: Practical Information 85
    Best Time to Visit 85
    Currency and Banking 87
    Health and Safety 89
    Visa and Entry Requirements 92
    Local Customs and Laws 95

CHAPTER 10: Day Trips and Excursions 98

CHAPTER 11: Shopping and Souvenirs 102
    Local Handicrafts 103

CHAPTER 12: Itineraries 106
    3-Day Itinerary 106
    7-Day Itinerary 107

Adventure Seeker's Itinerary 109
Family-Friendly Itinerary 110
Cultural Explorer's Itinerary 111
CONCLUSION 112

INTRODUCTION

I still remember the first time I set foot on the sun-drenched shores of Gibraltar. It was a crisp morning, the air was filled with a mix of salt from the sea and the tantalizing scent of fresh pastries from a nearby café. As I stepped off the plane and looked up, the imposing Rock of Gibraltar loomed above, its rugged cliffs kissed by the early morning sun. It was love at first sight.

My journey began with a leisurely stroll through the charming streets of the old town, where history whispered from every corner. Narrow alleyways led to bustling squares, each one alive with the vibrant colors and sounds of local life. My senses were immediately captivated by the blend of cultures that define this unique peninsula. British red phone boxes stood alongside Moorish architecture, and Spanish guitar music mingled with the calls of seagulls overhead.

The first sight that truly took my breath away was St. Michael's Cave. Descending into its cool depths, I felt like an explorer discovering a hidden world. The ethereal beauty of the stalactites and stalagmites, illuminated by a kaleidoscope of lights, was nothing short of magical. And then, stepping out onto the Mediterranean Steps, I was met with panoramic views that stretched from the African coast to the sprawling Spanish countryside. It was a moment of pure awe and wonder.

These initial impressions, so vivid and unforgettable, inspired me to delve deeper into the heart of Gibraltar. I wanted to uncover its secrets, to understand its soul, and to share these discoveries with fellow travelers. This guide is born out of that passion—a desire to connect others to the magic of Gibraltar.

Whether you're a first-time visitor eager to explore iconic landmarks, an adventure seeker looking for thrilling outdoor activities, or a family in search of memorable experiences, this guide is for you. It's crafted with love and filled with insider tips, local secrets, and practical advice to help you make the most of your visit.

In these pages, you'll find everything from the best spots to watch dolphins frolic in the bay to hidden eateries where you can savor traditional dishes. You'll learn about the rich history that has shaped Gibraltar and discover off-the-beaten-path gems that will leave you enchanted.

So, come along with me on this journey. Let's wander the ancient streets, climb to breathtaking heights, and dive into the crystal-clear waters together. Gibraltar is waiting to share its stories with you, and I can't wait for you to experience the magic for yourself.

Welcome to the Travel Guide To Gibraltar 2025—your ultimate companion to exploring this extraordinary corner of the world.

CHAPTER 1: Getting to Gibraltar

Flights and Airports

Welcome to Gibraltar, the stunning gateway to both Europe and Africa! Your journey begins at Gibraltar International Airport (GIB), a small but bustling hub that offers everything you need for a smooth and enjoyable arrival.

Gibraltar International Airport (GIB)
Nestled between the Rock of Gibraltar and the sea, Gibraltar International Airport is one of the most unique airports in the world. Despite its compact size, it boasts modern facilities including duty-free shopping, cozy cafes, and efficient baggage claim services. The airport's friendly staff are always on hand to assist you, ensuring a warm welcome as you embark on your adventure.

Airlines and Routes
- Several airlines operate flights to Gibraltar, making it accessible from various major cities. British Airways offers regular flights from London Heathrow, while easyJet connects Gibraltar with London Gatwick and Manchester. Additionally, Wizz Air provides seasonal flights from London Luton. These airlines ensure that whether you're coming from the UK or other European destinations, you have convenient options to reach Gibraltar.

Booking Flights and Finding Deals

Booking your flight to Gibraltar can be a breeze if you know where to look. Websites like Skyscanner, Kayak, and Google Flights are excellent resources for comparing prices and finding the best deals. Set up fare alerts to get notifications about price drops, and consider booking in advance, especially during peak travel seasons, to secure the best rates. Don't forget to check the airlines' official websites for exclusive offers and discounts!

Airport Transfers and Transportation

Once you've landed, getting to the city center is straightforward. The airport is just a short distance from the heart of Gibraltar, making transfers quick and easy. You can hop into a taxi right outside the terminal; the ride to the city center typically takes about 10 minutes and costs around £10.

For those who prefer public transportation, there are buses available that connect the airport to various parts of Gibraltar. Bus routes 5 and 10 are particularly handy, with frequent services to and from the city center. Alternatively, if you're up for a stroll, the city center is only a 20-minute walk away, allowing you to start soaking in the sights right from the get-go.

Ferry Connections

Arriving in Gibraltar by ferry is an adventurous and scenic way to start your journey. Let's explore the essential details to ensure your trip is smooth and enjoyable.

Ports Offering Ferry Services to Gibraltar

Ferry services to Gibraltar are primarily available from Morocco, specifically from the port of Tangier Med. This offers a fantastic opportunity to combine your visit to Gibraltar with a Moroccan adventure.

Booking Ferry Tickets and Checking Schedules

Booking your ferry tickets is straightforward. Websites like Direct Ferries and Ferryhopper allow you to compare prices, schedules, and book tickets online. It's a good idea to book in advance, especially during peak travel seasons, to secure your spot and get the best prices. Always check the schedules close to your departure date, as ferry times can sometimes change due to weather conditions.

Ferry Operators and Their Services

Several operators provide ferry services to Gibraltar, with FRS Ferries being one of the most prominent. FRS Ferries offers regular crossings from Tangier Med to Gibraltar, typically with a travel time of around 1.5 to 2 hours. The ferries are equipped with comfortable seating, refreshments, and even onboard entertainment to make your journey pleasant.

What to Expect During the Ferry Ride

The ferry ride to Gibraltar is not just a means of transport but an experience in itself. As you sail across the Strait of Gibraltar, you'll be treated to stunning views of both the European and African coastlines. Keep your camera handy—you might even spot dolphins playing in the waves!

Once onboard, you can relax in the lounge area, grab a snack or drink from the cafeteria, and enjoy the scenic journey. If the weather is nice, head out to the deck to breathe in the fresh sea air and take in the panoramic views.

Border Crossings from Spain

Traveling to Gibraltar from Spain is a seamless experience if you know what to expect. Here's a clear guide to help you navigate the border crossing with ease.

Border Crossing Process
The primary border crossing between Spain and Gibraltar is located at La Línea de la Concepción. This is a busy yet efficiently managed crossing point where travelers can enter Gibraltar either by foot, car, or public transportation. The process is usually straightforward, but being prepared can save you time.

Documents You Need
To cross the border, you'll need to present valid identification. Here's what you should bring:
Passport: Required for non-EU nationals and recommended for EU nationals for ease of identification.
National ID Card: Accepted for EU nationals.
Ensure your documents are up-to-date and easily accessible to expedite the process.
Specific Rules and Restrictions
Customs Regulations: Be aware of customs regulations when bringing goods into Gibraltar. Certain items like alcohol and tobacco have restrictions, so check current limits before crossing.
Vehicle Entry: If you're driving, ensure your car insurance covers Gibraltar. It's also a good idea to carry your vehicle registration and proof of insurance.
Getting to the Border Crossing from Nearby Spanish Cities

From Málaga: Take the AP-7 highway southwest towards La Línea de la Concepción. The drive takes approximately 1.5 to 2 hours.

From Seville: Head southeast on the A-4 and then switch to the A-381 towards La Línea. This journey typically takes about 2.5 to 3 hours.

From Cadiz: Travel southeast on the A-381 to reach La Línea in roughly 1.5 hours.

Clear signage will guide you to the border crossing as you approach La Línea.

Tips for Pedestrians, Drivers, and Public Transportation Users

Pedestrians: If you're crossing on foot, the pedestrian lane is clearly marked. Be prepared for a brief wait, especially during peak times. The walk from the border to Gibraltar's city center is around 15 minutes.

Drivers: When driving, follow the signs to the vehicle entry lanes. Traffic can be heavy, particularly during rush hours, so plan accordingly. Once through the border, there are several parking options in Gibraltar, but spaces can be limited.

Public Transportation Users: Buses and taxis frequently run between La Línea and the border. The bus station in La Línea is close to the crossing point, and regular services connect with nearby Spanish cities. Taxis can drop you right at the border crossing, making it a convenient option.

[handwritten: LA LINEA People get Free Bus Travel.]

CHAPTER 2: Getting Around

Public Transportation

Gibraltar's bus network is well-organized and covers most of the key areas, making it easy to get around. The main bus routes are:

Route 2: Runs from the border (La Línea) to Europa Point, passing through the city center and key attractions like the Gibraltar Museum and the Cathedral of St. Mary the Crowned.

Route 3: Connects the border with Rosia Bay, making stops at Main Street and the South District.

Route 4: Travels from the border to Upper Town, providing access to residential areas and schools.

Route 5: Links the city center with the Eastern Beach and Catalan Bay.

How to Use the Bus System

Using the bus system in Gibraltar is straightforward:

Paying Fares: You can pay your fare directly to the bus driver when you board. It's a good idea to carry some small change, as drivers may not always have enough change for larger bills.

Getting Tickets: Tickets can be purchased on the bus. Simply tell the driver your destination, and they will provide you with the appropriate ticket.

Contactless Payments: Many buses accept contactless payments, making it even more convenient.

Bus Schedules and Frequencies

Buses in Gibraltar run frequently, especially on popular routes. Here are some general guidelines:

Weekdays: Buses typically run every 15-20 minutes during peak hours and every 30 minutes during off-peak times.

Weekends and Public Holidays: Service may be less frequent, so it's a good idea to check the schedule in advance.

Car Rentals

Renting a car in Gibraltar offers the flexibility to explore at your own pace. Here's everything you need to know about renting and driving a car in this unique destination.

Car Rental Companies and Their Locations

Several car rental companies operate in Gibraltar, providing a variety of options to suit your needs:

Hertz: Located at Gibraltar International Airport and in the city center, Hertz offers a wide range of vehicles.

Avis: Situated near the airport, Avis provides convenient access for travelers arriving by air.

Budget: Also located at the airport, Budget is known for competitive pricing and a good selection of cars.

Europcar: Found in the city center, Europcar offers both short-term and long-term rentals.

Types of Vehicles Available for Rent

Car rental companies in Gibraltar offer a variety of vehicles, including:

Compact Cars: Ideal for navigating narrow city streets and finding parking easily.

Sedans: Suitable for families or small groups, offering more comfort and space.

SUVs: Perfect for those who need extra space or plan to venture into the countryside.

Luxury Cars: For those looking to travel in style, luxury options are available.

How to Book a Rental Car and What Documents Are Needed

Booking a rental car in Gibraltar is simple:

Online Reservations: Most car rental companies have websites where you can book your vehicle in advance. This ensures availability and often provides the best rates.

Walk-In Reservations: You can also visit the rental offices in person to book a car, though availability may be limited during peak seasons.

When booking a rental car, you will need:

Valid Driver's License: An international driving permit (IDP) is recommended if your license is not in English.

Passport: For identification purposes.

Credit Card: Required for the security deposit and payment.

Driving Rules and Regulations in Gibraltar

Driving in Gibraltar is straightforward, but there are a few key rules to keep in mind:

Drive on the Right: Unlike in the UK, Gibraltar follows the continental European system, driving on the right side of the road.

Speed Limits: The speed limit in urban areas is generally 50 km/h (31 mph), and 80 km/h (50 mph) on open roads, unless otherwise posted.
Seat Belts: Mandatory for all passengers.
Mobile Phones: Using a mobile phone while driving is prohibited unless you have a hands-free system.
Parking Regulations: Pay attention to parking signs and regulations to avoid fines. Some areas require a parking disc, which can be obtained from car rental companies or local shops.

Tips for Parking and Navigating Gibraltar's Roads

Parking: Parking can be challenging in the city center, especially during peak hours. Look for designated parking areas and consider using parking garages if available.
Narrow Streets: Gibraltar has many narrow, winding streets. Compact cars are recommended for easier navigation.
Traffic: Traffic can be heavy near the border crossing and in the city center, especially during rush hours. Plan your travel times accordingly.
Fuel Stations: There are a few fuel stations in Gibraltar, so refueling is convenient. Make sure to return the car with the agreed fuel level to avoid extra charges.

Walking and Cycling

Pedestrian-Friendly Areas and Walking Routes

Gibraltar is very pedestrian-friendly, with plenty of well-marked walking routes:

Main Street: The heart of Gibraltar's shopping and dining district, perfect for a leisurely stroll. Enjoy a mix of local shops, cafes, and historic buildings.

Ocean Village: A picturesque area by the marina, ideal for a relaxing walk along the waterfront, with plenty of restaurants and bars.

Upper Rock Nature Reserve: Offers several walking trails with stunning views, including the popular Mediterranean Steps, which take you through dramatic cliffs and lush greenery.

Tips for Navigating Gibraltar's Streets and Roads on Foot

Stay on Sidewalks: Where available, always use sidewalks. In areas without sidewalks, walk on the left side of the road facing oncoming traffic.

Crosswalks: Use pedestrian crossings where possible, and always wait for the green signal at traffic lights.

Stay Hydrated: Gibraltar's climate can be warm, so carry water, especially if you're planning a long walk or hike.

Wear Comfortable Shoes: The terrain can be hilly and uneven in places, so sturdy, comfortable footwear is recommended.

Bike Rental Options and Cycling Routes

Cycling is a fantastic way to explore Gibraltar, and there are several rental options available:

Bike Hire Gibraltar: Offers a range of bikes for rent, including electric bikes, making it easier to tackle Gibraltar's hilly terrain.

Gibraltar Bike Tours: Provides guided bike tours that include bike rental, giving you a local's perspective on the best routes and attractions.

Popular cycling routes include:

Europa Point: Cycle to the southernmost point of Gibraltar for stunning views across the Strait to Africa.

Eastern Beach to Catalan Bay: A scenic ride along the eastern coast, perfect for a relaxing beachside bike ride.

Upper Rock Nature Reserve: For more adventurous cyclists, the reserve offers challenging routes with rewarding views.

Safety Advice for Walkers and Cyclists

Helmets: Always wear a helmet when cycling, and consider additional protective gear if you're taking on challenging routes.

Visibility: Wear bright or reflective clothing, especially if you're walking or cycling in the early morning or late evening.

Road Awareness: Be mindful of traffic, especially in busy areas. Follow all traffic signs and signals.

CHAPTER 3: History and Culture

Historical Overview of Gibraltar

Gibraltar's history is a rich tapestry woven with strategic importance, cultural diversity, and resilient spirit. Let's embark on a journey through time to understand the key events and figures that have shaped this remarkable place.

Strategic Importance and Military History
Situated at the crossroads of Europe and Africa, Gibraltar has always been of immense strategic importance. Its location at the entrance of the Mediterranean Sea made it a prized possession for various empires and a critical military outpost. The towering Rock of Gibraltar provided a natural fortress, making it a focal point for naval power and trade routes.

Key Events and Periods in Gibraltar's Past
Moorish Occupation (711-1462): The Moors were the first to recognize Gibraltar's strategic significance. In 711 AD, Tariq ibn Ziyad led a Moorish force that landed on the Rock, marking the beginning of Muslim rule in the region. The name "Gibraltar" itself is derived from "Jebel Tariq" (Mount of Tariq).
Spanish Period (1462-1704): After centuries of Moorish control, Gibraltar was captured by the Spanish in 1462. It remained under Spanish rule for over two centuries, during which it was fortified and further developed.

British Rule (1704-Present): Gibraltar's modern history began in 1704 when an Anglo-Dutch fleet seized it during the War of the Spanish Succession. The Treaty of Utrecht in 1713 officially ceded Gibraltar to Britain. Since then, it has been a British Overseas Territory, playing a crucial role in British naval strategy, especially during the Napoleonic Wars and both World Wars.

Impact on Culture and Identity
Gibraltar's history has profoundly influenced its culture and identity. The blending of Moorish, Spanish, and British influences is evident in its architecture, language, and traditions. Gibraltarians speak both English and Llanito, a unique dialect that incorporates elements of English, Spanish, and other Mediterranean languages. This cultural mosaic creates a vibrant, cosmopolitan atmosphere that is distinctly Gibraltarian.

Important Historical Figures
Tariq ibn Ziyad: The Moorish general whose landing in 711 AD marked the beginning of Muslim rule in the region.
Admiral Sir George Rooke: Led the Anglo-Dutch fleet that captured Gibraltar in 1704.
General Eliott, Lord Heathfield: Defended Gibraltar during the Great Siege (1779-1783) when Spanish and French forces attempted to recapture it.

Modern History and Path to Autonomy
In the 20th century, Gibraltar's strategic importance was reaffirmed during World War II when it served as a key base for Allied operations in the Mediterranean. Post-war, Gibraltar began to forge a path toward greater self-

governance. In 1967, Gibraltarians voted overwhelmingly to remain under British sovereignty, rejecting Spanish claims.

The 2006 Constitution further solidified Gibraltar's autonomy, granting it self-governance in all matters except defense and foreign relations. Today, Gibraltar maintains its unique status as a British Overseas Territory, proud of its rich heritage and resilient identity.

Cultural Heritage and Traditions

Gibraltar's cultural heritage is a vibrant mosaic of British, Spanish, and Mediterranean influences, creating a unique and dynamic identity. This rich blend is reflected in its cuisine, music, art, and daily life, making Gibraltar a fascinating destination for any visitor.

A Unique Blend of Influences
Gibraltar's cultural fabric is woven from centuries of interaction between different civilizations. The British influence is prominent, visible in everything from the red phone boxes to the English-speaking locals. However, Gibraltar's proximity to Spain and its historical ties to the Mediterranean also play a significant role in shaping its cultural identity. This fusion results in a lively and welcoming atmosphere where diverse traditions coexist harmoniously.

Traditional Gibraltarian Cuisine, Music, and Art
Cuisine: Gibraltarian cuisine is a delightful blend of Mediterranean flavors with British and Spanish twists. Traditional dishes like calentita, a chickpea flour-based savory snack, and panissa, a fried version of calentita, are local favorites. The influence of neighboring Andalusia is evident in dishes like gazpacho and paella, while British staples like fish and chips are also popular. Don't miss trying the local seafood, fresh from the surrounding waters.

Music and Art: Music in Gibraltar is as diverse as its culture, with a mix of British pop, Spanish flamenco, and traditional folk music. The annual Gibraltar Music Festival showcases this diversity, attracting international and local artists. Art in Gibraltar often reflects its unique landscape and cultural history, with local artists drawing inspiration from the Rock, the sea, and the bustling town life. The Fine Arts Gallery and various local exhibitions provide a glimpse into the artistic soul of Gibraltar.

Local Way of Life, Customs, and Values
Gibraltarians are known for their warm hospitality and strong sense of community. Family plays a central role in daily life, and social gatherings are common. The pace of life is relaxed, with a Mediterranean emphasis on enjoying good food, good company, and the beautiful surroundings.

Local customs include the siesta, a midday break common in Mediterranean cultures, and the evening paseo, a leisurely walk often taken by families along Main Street or the marina. Religious traditions also play a significant role, with various Christian, Jewish, and Muslim festivals celebrated throughout the year.

Historic Landmarks, Monuments, and Cultural Institutions

Gibraltar is dotted with historic landmarks and cultural institutions that tell the story of its rich heritage:
The Rock of Gibraltar: A symbol of the territory, offering historical sites like the Moorish Castle and the Great Siege Tunnels.
St. Michael's Cave: An impressive natural grotto used for concerts and cultural events.

The Gibraltar Museum: Showcases the natural and cultural history of Gibraltar, including artifacts from its diverse past.
The Convent: The official residence of the Governor of Gibraltar, with a history dating back to the Franciscan friars in 1531.
Alameda Botanical Gardens: A tranquil spot that highlights the botanical heritage of the region.

Preservation and Celebration of Cultural Heritage
Gibraltar takes pride in preserving and celebrating its cultural heritage. Festivals and public holidays are vibrant displays of local traditions:
Gibraltar National Day: Celebrated on September 10th, this day sees the whole territory adorned in red and white, with parades, concerts, and fireworks.
Calentita Food Festival: A culinary event celebrating the diverse flavors of Gibraltar, held annually in Casemates Square.
Religious Festivals: Easter processions, the Jewish Hanukkah, and Muslim Eid celebrations reflect the religious diversity and tolerance in Gibraltar.

Festivals and Events

Popular Festivals

Gibraltar National Day (September 10th): The pinnacle of Gibraltar's festive calendar, National Day is a vibrant celebration of local identity and pride. The entire territory is adorned in red and white, and the day is filled with parades, concerts, and fireworks. Thousands gather in Casemates Square for a grand celebration, making it a must-experience event for any visitor.

Gibraltar International Jazz Festival (Late October): This annual festival attracts renowned jazz musicians from around the world. Held at various venues, including the stunning St. Michael's Cave, the festival offers a series of concerts, workshops, and jam sessions, creating a magical atmosphere for music lovers.

Unique Events

Gibraltar Fair (Late August): This traditional fair is a week-long event filled with amusement rides, games, and food stalls. It's a fantastic opportunity to experience local culture, try delicious Gibraltarian street food, and enjoy the lively atmosphere.

Candlelight Concert (Varies): Hosted in the magnificent setting of St. Michael's Cave, the Candlelight Concert features classical music performed by talented musicians. The cave's natural acoustics and candlelit ambiance make for an unforgettable musical experience.

Cultural Celebrations

Fiesta de la Mercè (September): Celebrated by the Catalan community in Gibraltar, this festival honors the Virgin of Mercy with processions, traditional dances, and music. It's a wonderful way to experience the cultural diversity within Gibraltar.

Eid al-Fitr (Varies): Marking the end of Ramadan, Eid al-Fitr is celebrated by Gibraltar's Muslim community with prayers, feasts, and gatherings. Visitors are often welcomed to join in the communal celebrations and experience the rich cultural tapestry of Gibraltar.

Tips for Enjoying Gibraltar's Festivals and Events

Plan Ahead: Many events, especially during peak tourist seasons, can get crowded. Book your accommodations and tickets in advance to secure your spot.

Join the Locals: Don't be shy—Gibraltarians are known for their hospitality. Engage with locals to get insider tips and truly immerse yourself in the festivities.

Dress Comfortably: Many festivals involve a lot of walking and standing, so wear comfortable shoes and clothing suitable for the weather.

Try Local Delicacies: Festivals are the perfect time to sample traditional Gibraltarian dishes from street vendors and food stalls.

Best Times of Year to Visit for Festivals and Events

Spring (March to May): This season sees pleasant weather and the beginning of outdoor events, including cultural festivals and street fairs.

Summer (June to August): A bustling time with major events like the Gibraltar Fair and various music festivals. The warm weather is perfect for outdoor celebrations.

Autumn (September to November): This period features some of the biggest events, including Gibraltar National Day and the International Jazz Festival, along with cooler, comfortable weather.

Winter (December to February): While quieter, winter still offers unique events and a festive atmosphere, especially around Christmas and New Year.

Cultural Etiquette

Local Customs and Traditions
Gibraltar is a melting pot of British, Spanish, and Mediterranean cultures, creating a distinctive blend of customs and traditions. Family and community are highly valued, and social gatherings are common. Gibraltarians are generally warm, friendly, and welcoming to visitors, so showing respect and politeness will go a long way.

Respecting Gibraltar's Cultural Heritage
Historical Sites: When visiting historical landmarks, such as the Moorish Castle or St. Michael's Cave, be respectful of the surroundings. Avoid touching artifacts and follow any guidelines provided by tour guides or signage.
Religious Sites: Respect the sanctity of churches, synagogues, and mosques. Dress modestly, keep noise levels low, and refrain from taking photographs unless permitted.

Dress Code, Table Manners, and Social Interactions
Dress Code: Gibraltar has a relaxed approach to dress, especially due to its warm climate. However, modest attire is appreciated in religious and formal settings. Swimwear is appropriate only at the beach or poolside.
Table Manners: Meals are often a social affair in Gibraltar. It's polite to wait for everyone to be served before starting your meal. When dining at a local's home, it's customary to bring a small gift, such as flowers or wine.
Social Interactions: Greetings typically involve a handshake, and close friends or family may greet with a kiss on each cheek. Maintain eye contact when speaking, as it shows sincerity and engagement.

Gestures, Body Language, and Communication Styles

Gestures: Common gestures such as a thumbs-up or a wave are understood, but avoid using overly dramatic hand gestures as they may be misinterpreted.

Body Language: Gibraltarians are generally comfortable with close personal space during conversations. Avoid crossing your arms, as it may be seen as defensive or unfriendly.

Communication Styles: English is the official language, but many locals also speak Spanish and Llanito (a mix of English, Spanish, and other Mediterranean languages). Politeness and respect are key in conversations. If you don't understand something, politely ask for clarification.

Avoiding Cultural Faux Pas and Making a Good Impression

Punctuality: While Gibraltarians are relatively relaxed about time, it's still respectful to be punctual for formal appointments or meetings.

Tipping: Tipping is appreciated but not obligatory. A 10-15% tip in restaurants and rounding up the fare for taxi drivers is customary.

Photography: Always ask for permission before taking photos of people, especially in private or sensitive settings.

Local Language and Phrases

Overview of Languages Spoken in Gibraltar

English: The official language of Gibraltar, used in government, education, and most public signage.

Spanish: Widely spoken due to Gibraltar's proximity to Spain and historical ties.

Llanito: A unique dialect blending English and Spanish with influences from Italian, Portuguese, and other Mediterranean languages. Llanito is commonly spoken among locals in casual settings.

Common Phrases and Expressions in Llanito and Spanish

Llanito:

"¿Qué pasa?" (keh pah-sah) – What's happening?

"Voy p'al trabajo" (boy pahl trah-bah-ho) – I'm going to work.

"¿Cómo estás?" (koh-moh eh-stahs) – How are you?

Spanish:

"Hola" (oh-lah) – Hello

"Buenos días" (bweh-nohs dee-ahs) – Good morning

"Gracias" (grah-see-ahs) – Thank you

"Por favor" (por fah-vor) – Please

"Perdón" (pehr-don) – Excuse me / Sorry

Helpful Words and Phrases for Visitors
Greetings and Polite Expressions:
"Hola" (oh-lah) – Hello
"Buenos días" (bweh-nohs dee-ahs) – Good morning
"Buenas tardes" (bweh-nahs tahr-dehs) – Good afternoon
"Buenas noches" (bweh-nahs noh-chehs) – Good evening / Good night
"Adiós" (ah-dee-ohs) – Goodbye
"Gracias" (grah-see-ahs) – Thank you
"De nada" (deh nah-dah) – You're welcome
"Por favor" (por fah-vor) – Please

Directions and Basic Questions:
"¿Dónde está...?" (dohn-deh eh-stah) – Where is...?
"¿Cómo llego a...?" (koh-moh yeh-goh ah) – How do I get to...?
"¿Cuánto cuesta?" (kwan-toh kwes-tah) – How much does it cost?
"¿Puede ayudarme?" (pweh-deh ah-yoo-dar-meh) – Can you help me?

Tips on Pronunciation and Understanding Local Accents

Pronunciation Tips:

Vowels: Spanish vowels are generally short and crisp. For example, "a" is pronounced like the "a" in "father," "e" like the "e" in "bet," "i" like the "ee" in "see," "o" like the "o" in "lot," and "u" like the "oo" in "food."

Stress: In Spanish, if a word ends in a vowel, "n," or "s," the stress is usually on the second-to-last syllable. If it ends in any other consonant, the stress is on the last syllable.

Understanding Local Accents:

Gibraltarians may switch between English, Spanish, and Llanito seamlessly. Pay attention to context and body language to aid comprehension.

Don't hesitate to ask locals to repeat themselves if you don't understand. They are generally friendly and happy to help.

Resources for Further Language Learning and Cultural Immersion

Language Apps: Apps like Duolingo, Babbel, and Rosetta Stone offer courses in both Spanish and English.

Local Classes: Look for language classes at community centers or local universities.

Cultural Immersion: Participate in local events, festivals, and markets to practice your language skills and experience the culture firsthand.

HOW TO USE THE QR CODE

We've added QR codes throughout this guide to make navigating easier. Here's how to use them:

1. Scan the QR Code using your smartphone's camera or a QR code scanner app.

2. Open in a Browser or on Google Maps app, for the best results.

3. View the Destination on the Google Maps page that opens. You'll find useful details like photos and reviews.

4. Tap "Directions" to get step-by-step guidance from your current location.

5. Follow the Route provided by Google Maps and enjoy your trip!

CHAPTER 4: Top Attractions

The Rock of Gibraltar

The Rock of Gibraltar is more than just a stunning geological formation; it's a symbol of the territory's rich history and strategic importance. Towering over the landscape at 426 meters (1,398 feet) above sea level, the Rock offers breathtaking views, fascinating historical sites, and diverse wildlife.

What to See and Do:

Cable Car Ride: Start your adventure with a scenic cable car ride from the base to the top of the Rock. The journey offers spectacular views of Gibraltar, the Mediterranean Sea, and even the African coastline on a clear day.

Address: Grand Parade, Gibraltar GX11 1AA

Hours: 9:30 AM - 7:15 PM (varies seasonally)

Fee: £16 (round trip for adults), £7.50 (round trip for children)

Apes' Den: Home to Gibraltar's famous Barbary macaques, Apes' Den is a must-visit. These cheeky, free-roaming monkeys are a delight to watch, but remember not to feed or touch them.

Address: Upper Rock Nature Reserve, Gibraltar

Hours: Accessible all day

Fee: Included in the Nature Reserve entrance fee

Skywalk: For thrill-seekers, the Skywalk offers a glass platform suspended high above the ground, providing stunning panoramic views.
Address: Upper Rock Nature Reserve, Gibraltar
Hours: Accessible all day
Fee: Included in the Nature Reserve entrance fee
Historical Significance:
The Rock has been a strategic military site for centuries, used by the Moors, Spaniards, and British. Its network of tunnels and fortifications played a crucial role during the Great Siege and World War II.

St. Michael's Cave
St. Michael's Cave is a natural wonder located within the Upper Rock Nature Reserve. This network of limestone caves is one of Gibraltar's most popular tourist attractions, known for its stunning formations and captivating history.

What to See and Do:
Stalactites and Stalagmites: Marvel at the intricate limestone formations that have developed over thousands of years.
Concert Hall: The main chamber of St. Michael's Cave has been transformed into a unique concert hall, hosting performances and events throughout the year. The natural acoustics and atmospheric lighting make for an unforgettable experience.
Lower St. Michael's Cave: For the adventurous, guided tours are available to explore the deeper sections of the cave,

offering a glimpse into its more remote and less-visited areas.
Details:
Address: Upper Rock Nature Reserve, Gibraltar
Hours: 9:30 AM - 6:15 PM
Fee: £12 (adults), £7 (children) – includes entrance to the Nature Reserve
Historical Significance:
Legend has it that the cave was once believed to be bottomless, with some even speculating that it was one of the entrances to the underworld. Archaeological findings suggest that the cave has been known to humans since prehistoric times.

Gibraltar Nature Reserve
The Gibraltar Nature Reserve, covering much of the Upper Rock, is a sanctuary for a wide variety of flora and fauna. This protected area offers a serene escape into nature, with numerous trails, lookout points, and historical sites.

What to See and Do:
Mediterranean Steps: A challenging yet rewarding hiking trail that takes you through some of the most scenic parts of the reserve, offering spectacular views along the way.
Upper Rock: Explore the Upper Rock's diverse wildlife, including the Barbary macaques, various bird species, and rare plants.

Military Heritage: Discover the historical military sites within the reserve, including old batteries and fortifications.
Details:
Address: Upper Rock, Gibraltar
Hours: 9:30 AM - 7:15 PM
Fee: £12 (adults), £7 (children)

Wildlife:
The reserve is home to the only wild monkey population in Europe, the Barbary macaques. Birdwatchers can also spot a variety of migratory birds, especially during the spring and autumn migrations.

Europa Point
Europa Point is the southernmost tip of Gibraltar, offering breathtaking views across the Strait of Gibraltar to Morocco. It's a perfect spot for sightseeing and soaking in the stunning surroundings.

What to See and Do:
Trinity Lighthouse: This iconic lighthouse has been guiding ships safely through the Strait since 1841. It's an excellent spot for photography.

Our Lady of Europe Shrine: A historical religious site that dates back to the 14th century, providing a peaceful place for reflection.

Harding's Battery: Explore this restored artillery battery, which offers insights into Gibraltar's military history.
Details:

Address: Europa Point, Gibraltar
Hours: Open 24 hours
Fee: Free
Activities:
Europa Point is also a popular spot for whale and dolphin watching. Various tour operators offer boat trips from the nearby marinas.

The Great Siege Tunnels
The Great Siege Tunnels, also known as the Upper Galleries, are a fascinating network of tunnels carved out during the Great Siege of Gibraltar in the late 18th century. They stand as a testament to the ingenuity and resilience of the British forces.

What to See and Do:
Tunnel Tours: Take a guided tour through the tunnels to learn about their construction and use during the siege. The tour includes detailed exhibits and displays of historical artifacts.
Viewpoints: The tunnels offer several strategic viewpoints overlooking the Bay of Gibraltar and the Spanish mainland. These were once crucial firing positions during the siege.
Details:
Address: Upper Rock Nature Reserve, Gibraltar
Hours: 9:00 AM - 6:00 PM
Fee: £12 (adults), £7 (children) – includes entrance to the Nature Reserve
Historical Significance:

The tunnels were dug out by hand using basic tools and explosives. Their creation was a remarkable engineering feat, providing crucial defensive positions and storage during the siege.

Moorish Castle

The Moorish Castle is a significant historical landmark in Gibraltar, offering a glimpse into the territory's rich past. Built in the early 8th century during the Moorish occupation, the castle complex includes the Tower of Homage and the Gate House.

What to See and Do:
Tower of Homage: The most prominent part of the castle, offering panoramic views of Gibraltar and the surrounding areas. Explore its ancient walls and imagine the historical battles fought here.
Gate House: The entrance to the castle complex, showcasing impressive Moorish architecture.
Details:

Address: Moorish Castle Estate, Gibraltar
Hours: 9:00 AM - 6:00 PM
Fee: £12 (adults), £7 (children) – includes entrance to the Nature Reserve
Historical Significance:
The castle played a crucial role during the Moorish occupation and subsequent battles between the Moors and Spanish forces.

Gibraltar Museum

The Gibraltar Museum offers a comprehensive look into the territory's history, from prehistoric times to the present day. It features fascinating exhibits on Gibraltar's natural history, archaeology, and cultural heritage.

What to See and Do:
Historical Exhibits: Explore artifacts from Gibraltar's past, including Roman and Moorish relics.
Rock Model: A detailed scale model of the Rock of Gibraltar, providing an overview of its topography and key landmarks.
Great Siege Gallery: Learn about the Great Siege of Gibraltar through interactive displays and historical artifacts.
Details:
Address: 18-20 Bomb House Lane, Gibraltar
Hours: 10:00 AM - 6:00 PM (Monday to Friday), 10:00 AM - 2:00 PM (Saturday)
Fee: £5 (adults), £2.50 (children)

Trafalgar Cemetery
Trafalgar Cemetery is a historic cemetery located near the southern entrance of Main Street. It is named in honor of the Battle of Trafalgar, although only two of the casualties from the battle are buried here. The cemetery is the final resting place for many who died in the early 19th century.

What to See and Do:

Historical Gravestones: Wander through the cemetery and read the inscriptions on the gravestones, each telling a story of Gibraltar's past.

Memorials: Pay your respects at the memorials dedicated to those who fought in the Battle of Trafalgar and other conflicts.

Details:

Address: Trafalgar Road, Gibraltar

Hours: 9:00 AM - 7:00 PM

Fee: Free

Historical Significance:

The cemetery is a poignant reminder of Gibraltar's military history and the many lives affected by conflict.

CHAPTER 5: Hidden Gems and Off-the-Beaten-Path

Gorham's Cave Complex

Gorham's Cave Complex is a UNESCO World Heritage site that offers a fascinating glimpse into prehistoric human life. The caves were inhabited by Neanderthals over 40,000 years ago, making them one of the last known refuges of this ancient species.

What to See and Do:

Guided Tours: Explore the caves with a knowledgeable guide who can provide insights into the archaeological findings and significance of the site.

Visitor Center: Learn more about the history and excavation efforts through informative displays and exhibits.

Details:

Address: Mediterranean Steps, Gibraltar

Hours: Tours are by appointment only

Fee: £20 (adults), £10 (children) – guided tours

Historical Significance:

The site has provided invaluable insights into Neanderthal life, including evidence of hunting, tool use, and possibly symbolic behavior.

Catalan Bay

Catalan Bay is a charming fishing village located on the eastern side of Gibraltar. Known for its picturesque setting and colorful houses, it's a perfect spot to experience local culture and enjoy the seaside.

What to See and Do:

Beach: Relax on the sandy beach, swim in the clear waters, or enjoy water sports.

Local Cuisine: Savor fresh seafood at one of the village's quaint restaurants or cafes.

Photography: Capture stunning photos of the brightly colored houses and the serene bay.

Details:

Address: Catalan Bay, Gibraltar

Hours: Accessible all day

Fee: Free

Cultural Significance:

The village has a rich cultural heritage, with a community that has maintained traditional fishing practices for generations.

Windsor Suspension Bridge

The Windsor Suspension Bridge is a spectacular 71-meter-long (233 feet) pedestrian bridge that offers breathtaking views of the surrounding landscape. It's part of the Upper Rock Nature Reserve and provides a thrilling experience for visitors.

What to See and Do:

Bridge Walk: Enjoy a walk across the bridge, taking in the stunning views of the Rock, the city below, and the Strait of Gibraltar.
Hiking Trails: Combine your visit with a hike on one of the nearby trails for a full day of adventure and nature.
Details:
Address: Upper Rock Nature Reserve, Gibraltar
Hours: Accessible all day
Fee: Included in the Nature Reserve entrance fee
Adventure Factor:
The bridge offers a unique vantage point and a bit of thrill, especially on windy days when you can feel it gently sway.

Alameda Wildlife Conservation Park

The Alameda Wildlife Conservation Park is a small but charming zoo located within the Alameda Botanical Gardens. It's home to a variety of rescued animals and offers a delightful experience for families and animal lovers.

What to See and Do:

Animal Exhibits: See a range of animals, from exotic birds and reptiles to small mammals, all housed in naturalistic enclosures.

Educational Programs: Participate in educational programs and talks to learn more about the conservation efforts and the animals' stories.

Botanical Gardens: Explore the surrounding botanical gardens, which showcase a variety of native and exotic plant species.

Details:

Address: Red Sands Road, Gibraltar

Hours: 10:00 AM - 5:00 PM (Monday to Friday), 10:00 AM - 4:00 PM (Saturday and Sunday)

Fee: £5 (adults), £2.50 (children)

Conservation Efforts:

The park focuses on the rescue and rehabilitation of animals, promoting conservation and environmental education.

Jews' Gate Cemetery

Jews' Gate Cemetery is a historic Jewish cemetery located at the southern end of the Upper Rock Nature Reserve. It offers a peaceful and reflective space, rich with history.

What to See and Do:

Gravestones: Walk among the ancient gravestones, many of which date back to the 18th and 19th centuries, and read the inscriptions that tell the stories of Gibraltar's Jewish community.

Historical Significance: Learn about the history of the Jewish community in Gibraltar, which has played a

significant role in the territory's cultural and economic development.
Details:
Address: Jews' Gate, Upper Rock Nature Reserve, Gibraltar
Hours: 9:00 AM - 6:00 PM
Fee: Included in the Nature Reserve entrance fee
Cultural Significance:
The cemetery is an important historical site, reflecting the long-standing presence and contributions of the Jewish community in Gibraltar.

Mediterranean Steps

The Mediterranean Steps offer a challenging yet rewarding hiking experience, taking you through some of Gibraltar's most scenic and rugged terrain. This steep trail provides breathtaking views of the Mediterranean Sea and the surrounding landscapes.

What to See and Do:
Hiking: Tackle the steep and winding steps, which are part of a historic path used by military personnel.
Scenic Views: Enjoy panoramic views of the coastline, the Rock, and on clear days, the African coast.
Nature: Encounter diverse flora and fauna, including rare plants and bird species.
Details:
Address: Upper Rock Nature Reserve, Gibraltar
Hours: Accessible all day
Fee: Included in the Nature Reserve entrance fee
Adventure Factor:

The hike is quite demanding, so be prepared with sturdy shoes, water, and sun protection. The effort is well worth the spectacular views and sense of accomplishment.

Parson's Lodge Battery
Parson's Lodge Battery is a historic coastal fortification located at Rosia Bay. Built in the 19th century, it played a crucial role in the defense of Gibraltar's waters.
What to See and Do:
Historic Fort: Explore the well-preserved fort, which includes gun emplacements, tunnels, and barracks.
Educational Displays: Learn about the military history of Gibraltar and the strategic importance of Rosia Bay.
Scenic Spot: Enjoy the views of the bay and the surrounding area, making it a peaceful spot for photography and reflection.
Details:
Address: Rosia Bay, Gibraltar
Hours: 10:00 AM - 6:00 PM
Fee: Free

Historical Significance:
Parson's Lodge Battery is a testament to Gibraltar's military past and its strategic significance in controlling access to the Mediterranean.

City Under Siege Exhibition
The City Under Siege Exhibition provides a fascinating look into the lives of Gibraltarians during the Great Siege of 1779-1783. This interactive museum is housed in one of the old bastions of Gibraltar's defenses.

What to See and Do:
Interactive Exhibits: Experience what life was like during the siege through detailed exhibits, dioramas, and multimedia presentations.
Historical Artifacts: View artifacts from the siege, including weapons, uniforms, and personal items of soldiers and civilians.
Educational Experience: Gain a deeper understanding of the hardships and resilience of Gibraltar's inhabitants during one of its most challenging periods.

Details:
Address: Upper Rock Nature Reserve, Gibraltar
Hours: 9:00 AM - 6:00 PM
Fee: Included in the Nature Reserve entrance fee

Cultural Insight:
The exhibition offers a poignant reminder of Gibraltar's strategic importance and the bravery of its people during times of conflict.

The Shrine of Our Lady of Europe
The Shrine of Our Lady of Europe is a historic and religious site located at Europa Point. This shrine has been a place of pilgrimage and devotion for centuries.

What to See and Do:
Historic Chapel: Visit the chapel, which dates back to the 14th century and contains beautiful religious art and artifacts.
Statue of Our Lady of Europe: Admire the statue of the Virgin Mary, which is a focal point of the shrine and holds great significance for the local Catholic community.
Peaceful Reflection: Enjoy the serene atmosphere and the stunning views of the Strait of Gibraltar.

Details:
Address: Europa Point, Gibraltar
Hours: 9:00 AM - 6:00 PM
Fee: Free

Cultural Significance:
The shrine reflects Gibraltar's rich religious heritage and the enduring faith of its people. It is a symbol of peace and unity, welcoming visitors of all backgrounds.

CHAPTER 6: Outdoor Activities

Gibraltar is a fantastic destination for rock climbing enthusiasts, offering a variety of routes that cater to all skill levels. The stunning natural landscape and panoramic views make climbing here an unforgettable experience.

Rock of Gibraltar Climbing Routes
The Rock of Gibraltar offers numerous climbing routes, ranging from beginner-friendly to challenging climbs for experienced climbers.
What to See and Do:
Climbing Routes: Explore popular climbing spots such as "The Great North Face" and "Upper Rock Crags," which provide a range of difficulties and breathtaking views.
Guided Climbs: Join a guided climbing tour for expert advice and safety. Local guides can show you the best routes and ensure a safe climbing experience.
Bouldering: For those who prefer bouldering, there are several spots with shorter climbs and challenging problems to solve.
Details:
Address: Various locations on the Rock of Gibraltar
Hours: Accessible all day, but early mornings or late afternoons are recommended to avoid the heat
Fee: Free (guided tours may have fees)
Climbing Tips:
- Ensure you have the proper equipment, including climbing shoes, harness, helmet, and ropes.

- Check weather conditions before heading out, as Gibraltar can get quite hot.
- Stay hydrated and bring plenty of water.
- Be mindful of local wildlife, including the Barbary macaques, who might be curious about climbers.

Climbing at Mediterranean Steps
The Mediterranean Steps offer another exciting climbing opportunity, combining a challenging hike with some climbing sections. This route provides stunning coastal views and a rewarding sense of adventure.

What to See and Do:
Hiking and Climbing: The Mediterranean Steps trail includes sections where you'll need to scramble and climb, making it an exciting combination of hiking and rock climbing.
Scenic Views: Enjoy breathtaking views of the Mediterranean Sea, the coastline, and even the African continent on clear days.
Wildlife Spotting: The area is home to diverse flora and fauna, so keep an eye out for interesting plants and animals along the way.
Details:
Address: Upper Rock Nature Reserve, Gibraltar
Hours: Accessible all day
Fee: Included in the Nature Reserve entrance fee
Climbing Tips:
- Wear sturdy hiking boots with good grip to handle the rocky terrain.

- Bring a map or GPS device to stay on the trail, as some sections can be tricky to navigate.
- Take your time and enjoy the scenery, as the climb can be strenuous but incredibly rewarding.

Safety Advice:
- Always climb with a partner or in a group for safety.
- Inform someone about your climbing plans and estimated return time.
- Carry a first aid kit and know basic first aid procedures.
- Respect the natural environment and leave no trace.

Bird Watching

Bird Observatory at Jews' Gate

The Bird Observatory at Jews' Gate is a fantastic spot for avid bird watchers. Managed by the Gibraltar Ornithological & Natural History Society (GONHS), this observatory provides excellent facilities and prime viewing opportunities.

What to See and Do:

Bird Watching: Observe a wide range of bird species, including raptors, songbirds, and waterfowl, particularly during the spring and autumn migrations.

Educational Programs: Participate in educational programs and workshops on bird conservation and identification offered by GONHS.

Guided Tours: Join guided bird-watching tours led by experienced ornithologists who can provide insights into the bird species and their behaviors.

Details:

Address: Jews' Gate, Upper Rock Nature Reserve, Gibraltar

Hours: Accessible during daylight hours; peak bird-watching times are early morning and late afternoon

Fee: Included in the Nature Reserve entrance fee

Bird Watching Tips:
- Bring binoculars and a bird identification guide to enhance your experience.
- Wear neutral-colored clothing to avoid startling the birds.
- Stay quiet and move slowly to increase your chances of spotting birds up close.

Europa Point Birdwatching

Europa Point is another excellent location for bird watching in Gibraltar. This southernmost point offers stunning views and the chance to see a variety of bird species, especially during migration periods.

What to See and Do:
Bird Watching: Look out for seabirds, raptors, and other migratory birds as they cross the Strait of Gibraltar. Species commonly seen include the Cory's shearwater, the osprey, and the honey buzzard.
Scenic Views: Enjoy the breathtaking scenery of the Mediterranean Sea and the distant African coastline while watching for birds.
Whale and Dolphin Watching: Combine your bird-watching trip with the possibility of spotting marine life, as Europa Point is also a popular spot for observing whales and dolphins.
Details:
Address: Europa Point, Gibraltar
Hours: Accessible all day; best bird-watching times are during migration seasons (spring and autumn)
Fee: Free

Bird Watching Tips:
- Use a spotting scope for a better view of distant birds.
- Check migration timetables to plan your visit during peak bird-watching periods.
- Bring a camera with a telephoto lens to capture close-up images of the birds.

Safety and Etiquette:
- Respect the natural environment and the wildlife by keeping a safe distance from the birds.
- Do not disturb nesting sites or feeding areas.
- Follow any guidelines or regulations provided by local authorities or conservation organizations.

Dolphin and Whale Watching Tours

Dolphin Adventure Tours

Dolphin Adventure Tours is one of Gibraltar's leading operators, providing memorable dolphin and whale watching experiences. With knowledgeable guides and comfortable boats, these tours are perfect for all ages.

What to See and Do:

Dolphin Watching: Encounter playful pods of common dolphins, striped dolphins, and bottlenose dolphins. The guides provide insightful commentary about the dolphins' behaviors and habitat.

Whale Watching: Depending on the season, you might spot orcas, pilot whales, and even sperm whales.

Scenic Boat Ride: Enjoy a scenic cruise through the Strait of Gibraltar, offering stunning views of the coastline and the Rock of Gibraltar.

Details:

Address: Marina Bay Square, Ocean Village, Gibraltar
Hours: Tours typically run multiple times daily; check the schedule for availability
Fee: £25 (adults), £15 (children)
Tour Tips:
- Bring a camera and binoculars for the best viewing experience.
- Wear sunscreen and a hat, and bring a light jacket as it can get breezy on the water.
- Arrive early to secure a good spot on the boat.

Dolphin Safari Gibraltar
Dolphin Safari Gibraltar offers another fantastic option for dolphin and whale watching tours. With a strong emphasis on conservation and education, Dolphin Safari provides an enriching and enjoyable experience.

What to See and Do:
Dolphin Watching: Spot various dolphin species, including the common dolphin and the bottlenose dolphin, known for their acrobatic displays and social behavior.
Whale Watching: Keep an eye out for larger cetaceans, such as pilot whales and orcas, especially during their migration periods.
Educational Experience: Learn about marine life, conservation efforts, and the ecological significance of the Strait of Gibraltar from expert guides.
Details:
Address: Marina Bay, Ocean Village, Gibraltar
Hours: Tours are available several times a day; check the website for exact timings

Fee: £27 (adults), £17 (children)

Tour Tips:
- Book your tour in advance to secure a spot, especially during peak tourist season.
- Follow the guides' instructions and maintain a safe distance from the animals to ensure their well-being.
- Be prepared for an awe-inspiring experience and the possibility of seeing other marine wildlife, such as sea turtles and various seabirds.

Safety and Etiquette:
- Always listen to the safety briefing provided by the tour operators.
- Avoid making loud noises or sudden movements that might disturb the marine animals.
- Respect the natural environment by not littering and following all guidelines provided by the tour operators.

Hiking Trails

Mediterranean Steps

The Mediterranean Steps trail is one of the most popular and challenging hikes in Gibraltar. This historic path, used by military personnel, offers breathtaking views and a rewarding hiking experience.

What to See and Do:
Steep Ascent: The trail includes a series of steep steps carved into the rock, leading hikers up the rugged terrain of the Upper Rock.
Scenic Views: Enjoy panoramic views of the Mediterranean Sea, the Strait of Gibraltar, and the African coast on clear days.
Flora and Fauna: Encounter diverse plant species and wildlife, including the famous Barbary macaques.
Details:
Address: Upper Rock Nature Reserve, Gibraltar
Hours: Accessible all day
Fee: Included in the Nature Reserve entrance fee
Hiking Tips:
- Wear sturdy hiking boots with good grip to handle the rocky terrain.
- Bring plenty of water, especially during warmer months.
- Start early in the morning to avoid the midday heat.
- Take your time and enjoy the stunning views along the way.

Upper Rock Nature Reserve Trails

The Upper Rock Nature Reserve offers several well-marked trails that cater to different fitness levels and interests. These trails provide an excellent way to explore Gibraltar's natural beauty and historical sites.

What to See and Do:

Historic Sites: Many trails lead to or pass by historical landmarks such as the Great Siege Tunnels, the Moorish Castle, and World War II fortifications.

Diverse Trails: Choose from a range of trails, including easy walks and more strenuous hikes. Popular trails include the Inglis Way, which offers gentle slopes and scenic views, and the Spur Battery Trail, which provides a more challenging hike with historical insights.

Wildlife Watching: Keep an eye out for Gibraltar's unique wildlife, including the Barbary macaques, various bird species, and butterflies.

Details:

Address: Upper Rock, Gibraltar

Hours: 9:00 AM - 7:00 PM (hours may vary seasonally)

Fee: £12 (adults), £7 (children) – includes entrance to the Nature Reserve

Hiking Tips:
- Carry a map or GPS device to stay on the designated trails.
- Wear comfortable clothing and appropriate footwear.
- Pack a snack and enjoy a picnic at one of the scenic viewpoints.
- Be mindful of the weather and check for any trail closures or advisories before setting out.

Safety and Etiquette:
- Stay on marked trails to protect the natural environment and avoid getting lost.
- Do not feed or disturb the wildlife, particularly the Barbary macaques.
- Take your litter with you and help keep the trails clean.
- Inform someone about your hiking plans and estimated return time for safety.

Scuba Diving and Snorkeling

Rosia Bay

Rosia Bay is a historic bay known for its clear waters and excellent diving conditions. The bay has significant historical relevance as it was the site where the damaged HMS Victory was anchored after the Battle of Trafalgar.

What to See and Do:

Scuba Diving: Explore the underwater world, which includes shipwrecks, reefs, and diverse marine life. Popular dive sites include the wrecks of SS Excellent and SS Rosslyn.

Snorkeling: The calm, clear waters of Rosia Bay make it ideal for snorkeling. Discover colorful fish, seaweed forests, and rock formations close to the shore.

Historic Sites: Above water, visit the Rosia Bay Heritage Trail to learn more about the area's maritime history.

Details:

Address: Rosia Bay, Gibraltar

Hours: Accessible all day

Fee: Free entry; diving tours may have fees

Diving and Snorkeling Tips:

- Use a reputable dive operator if you're not familiar with the area.
- Always dive with a buddy and follow standard safety protocols.
- Wear a wetsuit as the water can be cool, even in summer.
- Respect marine life and avoid touching or disturbing underwater habitats.

Camp Bay

Camp Bay is another popular spot for diving and snorkeling in Gibraltar. This area is known for its artificial reefs and rich biodiversity, providing an exciting underwater adventure.

What to See and Do:

Scuba Diving: Dive among artificial reefs created from sunken ships, concrete blocks, and other structures that attract a variety of marine species. The bay is home to octopuses, cuttlefish, and numerous fish species.

Snorkeling: The shallow areas of Camp Bay are perfect for snorkeling. Explore the vibrant underwater ecosystem, where you can see an array of marine life and interesting rock formations.

Beach Amenities: Enjoy the beach facilities, including picnic areas, showers, and a nearby beach bar for refreshments after your dive or snorkel.

Details:

Address: Camp Bay, Gibraltar

Hours: Accessible all day

Fee: Free entry; diving tours may have fees

Diving and Snorkeling Tips:
- Check local tide schedules and weather conditions before heading out.
- Bring your own snorkeling gear or rent from local shops if needed.
- Be mindful of boat traffic in the area and use a dive flag when diving.
- Take care to avoid sharp rocks and sea urchins while snorkeling.

Safety and Etiquette:
- Ensure you are adequately trained and equipped for diving, and always follow dive safety guidelines.
- Protect the marine environment by not touching coral or marine life and avoiding the collection of shells or other natural souvenirs.
- Dispose of any trash properly and help keep the beaches and waters clean.
- Respect other beachgoers and divers, and share the space responsibly.

Kayaking and Paddleboarding

Kayak Hire at Sandy Bay
Sandy Bay is a beautiful and serene spot on the eastern side of Gibraltar, perfect for kayaking. The sheltered waters and scenic surroundings make it a great location for both beginners and experienced kayakers.

What to See and Do:
Kayaking: Rent a kayak and paddle along the coastline, exploring hidden coves, sea caves, and rocky outcrops. Enjoy the tranquility of the bay and the stunning views of the Mediterranean Sea.
Wildlife Watching: Keep an eye out for marine life such as dolphins, fish, and seabirds as you paddle through the clear waters.
Beach Relaxation: After your kayaking adventure, relax on the sandy beach and take in the beautiful surroundings.
Details:
Address: Sandy Bay, Gibraltar
Hours: 9:00 AM - 6:00 PM (rental hours may vary)
Fee: Kayak rental fees vary; typically around £15-£20 per hour
Kayaking Tips:
- Wear a life jacket at all times and ensure it is properly fitted.
- Bring water, sunscreen, and a hat to protect yourself from the sun.
- Secure your belongings in a waterproof bag to keep them dry.

- Check the weather conditions and tide schedules before heading out.

Paddleboarding at Eastern Beach

Eastern Beach is another excellent location for water sports in Gibraltar. The calm and shallow waters make it an ideal spot for paddleboarding, offering a fun and relaxing way to explore the coastline.

What to See and Do:
Paddleboarding: Rent a paddleboard and glide across the gentle waves of Eastern Beach. The clear waters provide excellent visibility, allowing you to see the marine life below.
Scenic Views: Enjoy panoramic views of the coastline, the Rock of Gibraltar, and the open sea as you paddle along the beach.
Beach Amenities: Take advantage of the beach facilities, including restrooms, showers, and nearby cafes for a refreshing break.
Details:
Address: Eastern Beach, Gibraltar
Hours: 9:00 AM - 6:00 PM (rental hours may vary)
Fee: Paddleboard rental fees vary; typically around £15-£20 per hour
Paddleboarding Tips:
- Start on your knees to get a feel for the balance before standing up.
- Keep your feet shoulder-width apart and use your core muscles to maintain balance.

- Paddle on both sides to steer and keep a steady pace.
- Wear a leash attached to your ankle to prevent losing the board if you fall off.

Safety and Etiquette:
- Always be aware of your surroundings and other water users, including swimmers and boats.
- Respect marine life and avoid disturbing wildlife habitats.
- Follow any local regulations and guidelines provided by rental operators.
- Dispose of any trash properly and help keep the beaches and waters clean.

CHAPTER 7: Accommodation

Luxury Hotels

Sunborn Gibraltar
The Sunborn Gibraltar is a luxurious super-yacht hotel moored in Ocean Village Marina. This floating hotel offers an unparalleled experience with stunning views, elegant interiors, and top-notch amenities.
Details:
Address: Ocean Village Marina, Gibraltar GX11 1AA
Price Range: £250 - £500 per night
Highlights:
Stunning Views: Enjoy panoramic views of the marina, the Rock, and the Mediterranean Sea.
Luxurious Amenities: Indulge in the spa, take a dip in the rooftop pool, or try your luck at the casino.
Gourmet Dining: Savor exquisite cuisine at the hotel's fine dining restaurants.

The Rock Hotel
The Rock Hotel is an iconic and historic hotel perched on the cliffs of Gibraltar, offering breathtaking views and classic elegance. It has hosted many distinguished guests since it opened in 1932.
Details:

Address: 3 Europa Road, Gibraltar GX11 1AA
Price Range: £150 - £300 per night
Highlights:
Historic Charm: Experience the elegance and heritage of one of Gibraltar's most famous hotels.
Panoramic Views: Enjoy stunning vistas of the Strait of Gibraltar and the African coastline.
Beautiful Gardens: Relax in the hotel's beautifully landscaped gardens.

Boutique Hotels

The Eliott Hotel

The Eliott Hotel is a stylish boutique hotel located in the heart of Gibraltar. With its contemporary design and excellent service, it offers a comfortable and chic stay for travelers.

Details:
Address: 2 Governors Parade, Gibraltar GX11 1AA
Price Range: £120 - £250 per night
Highlights:
Central Location: Perfectly situated for exploring Gibraltar's main attractions and shopping areas.
Rooftop Pool: Enjoy a swim with a view at the rooftop pool.
Modern Comforts: Experience contemporary design and amenities in a stylish setting.

Budget-Friendly Options

Bristol Hotel

The Bristol Hotel is a historic and budget-friendly option located in the heart of Gibraltar. Known for its classic charm and convenient location, it offers a comfortable stay without breaking the bank.

Details:

Address: 8/10 Cathedral Square, Gibraltar GX11 1AA

Price Range: £70 - £120 per night

Highlights:

Central Location: Situated close to Main Street, providing easy access to shopping, dining, and attractions.

Outdoor Pool: Enjoy a refreshing dip in the outdoor pool, a rarity for budget accommodations.

Historic Charm: Experience the charm of one of Gibraltar's oldest hotels.

Cannon Hotel

The Cannon Hotel is another affordable option, offering simple yet comfortable accommodations. Its central location makes it a convenient base for exploring Gibraltar.

Details:

Address: 9 Cannon Lane, Gibraltar GX11 1AA

Price Range: £60 - £100 per night

Highlights:

Budget-Friendly: One of the most affordable hotels in Gibraltar, ideal for budget-conscious travelers.

Central Location: Close to Main Street, shops, and restaurants, making it easy to explore the city on foot.
Cozy Atmosphere: A small, friendly hotel with a welcoming atmosphere.

Emile Hostel
For those who prefer a hostel experience, Emile Hostel provides affordable dormitory and private room options. It's ideal for backpackers and solo travelers.
Details:
Address: 48 Irish Town, Gibraltar GX11 1AA
Price Range: £20 - £50 per night (depending on room type)
Highlights:
Budget-Friendly: Extremely affordable, making it perfect for budget travelers.
Social Atmosphere: Great for meeting other travelers and sharing experiences.

Family-Friendly Stays

Holiday Inn Express Gibraltar
Holiday Inn Express Gibraltar is an excellent choice for families, offering comfortable accommodations and convenient amenities that cater to both parents and children.
Details:
Address: 21-23 Devil's Tower Road, Gibraltar GX11 1AA
Price Range: £90 - £150 per night

Highlights:
Family Rooms: Spacious family rooms equipped with all the necessary amenities for a comfortable stay.
Complimentary Breakfast: Enjoy a free breakfast to start your day, perfect for fueling up before exploring Gibraltar.
Convenient Location: Located near popular attractions and within easy reach of the city center.

The O'Callaghan Eliott Hotel

The O'Callaghan Eliott Hotel is another family-friendly option, offering a blend of comfort, style, and convenience for families visiting Gibraltar.

Details:
Address: 2 Governors Parade, Gibraltar GX11 1AA
Price Range: £120 - £250 per night
Highlights:
Family Suites: Comfortable and spacious family suites that provide ample space for everyone.
Rooftop Pool: A rooftop pool where families can relax and enjoy the views after a day of sightseeing.
Central Location: Situated in the heart of Gibraltar, making it easy to access major attractions, shopping, and dining options.

Romantic Getaways

The Rock Hotel Suites
The Rock Hotel, with its timeless elegance and breathtaking views, offers luxurious suites that provide the perfect setting for a romantic getaway.
Details:
Address: 3 Europa Road, Gibraltar GX11 1AA
Price Range: £250 - £400 per night
Highlights:
Panoramic Views: Enjoy stunning views of the Strait of Gibraltar and the African coastline from the comfort of your suite.

Private Balconies: Many suites feature private balconies where you can relax and take in the scenery.

Historic Charm: The hotel's historic charm and beautiful gardens create a romantic and serene atmosphere.

Fine Dining: Experience exquisite dining at the hotel's restaurant, offering a romantic ambiance and delicious cuisine.

Sunborn Gibraltar Luxury Suites
The Sunborn Gibraltar, a super-yacht hotel, offers opulent luxury suites that are perfect for a romantic escape. Moored in Ocean Village Marina, this unique hotel provides an unparalleled experience.
Details:
Address: Ocean Village Marina, Gibraltar GX11 1AA
Price Range: £300 - £600 per night

Highlights:

Luxurious Suites: Indulge in spacious and elegantly designed suites with top-of-the-line amenities.

Stunning Views: Enjoy panoramic views of the marina, the Rock, and the Mediterranean Sea from your private terrace.

Rooftop Pool: Take a dip in the rooftop pool and relax on the sun deck with your partner.

Spa Services: Pamper yourselves with a range of spa treatments available at the onboard spa.

Gourmet Dining: Dine at the hotel's fine dining restaurant, offering a romantic setting and gourmet cuisine.

CHAPTER 8: Dining and Cuisine

Must-Try Dishes

Calentita
Calentita is one of Gibraltar's most iconic dishes, often considered the national dish. This simple yet delicious snack is made from chickpea flour, water, olive oil, and a pinch of salt, then baked to create a golden, crusty top with a soft, creamy interior.

Details:
Description: A baked chickpea flour pancake, similar to Italian farinata or French socca.
Flavor Profile: Slightly nutty and savory, with a rich and creamy texture.
Where to Try: Available at local bakeries, cafes, and during festivals such as the Calentita Food Festival.

Panissa
Panissa is another traditional Gibraltarian dish made from chickpea flour, but it's prepared differently from calentita. It's boiled, allowed to set, then cut into strips or shapes and fried until crispy.

Details:
Description: Fried chickpea flour sticks or slices, often enjoyed as a snack or side dish.
Flavor Profile: Crispy on the outside, soft on the inside, with a mild, savory taste.

Where to Try: Found in local tapas bars and cafes, often served with a sprinkling of sea salt.

Rosto

Rosto is a beloved pasta dish in Gibraltar, reflecting its Italian influence. It typically consists of pasta (usually penne or macaroni) tossed in a rich tomato sauce with carrots, onions, garlic, and minced beef or pork, sometimes topped with grated cheese.

Details:

Description: A hearty pasta dish with a flavorful tomato and meat sauce.

Flavor Profile: Savory and comforting, with the sweetness of carrots and richness of the meat sauce.

Where to Try: Served in many family-run restaurants and local eateries, especially those offering traditional Gibraltarian cuisine.

Traditional Tavernas

Roy's Cod Place

Roy's Cod Place is a beloved spot in Gibraltar known for its authentic British fish and chips, enhanced with a Mediterranean touch. This taverna is perfect for those looking to enjoy a hearty meal in a welcoming atmosphere.

Details:
Address: 123 Main Street, Gibraltar GX11 1AA
Price Range: £10 - £20 per meal

Highlights:
Signature Dish: Fish and chips, featuring fresh, locally sourced fish coated in a crispy batter and served with golden fries.
Casual Atmosphere: Enjoy a relaxed and friendly setting, ideal for a laid-back meal with family or friends.
Local Favorite: Popular among locals and tourists alike for its consistently delicious food and warm service.

Charlie's Tavern

Charlie's Tavern is a cozy and inviting establishment offering a variety of traditional Gibraltarian and Mediterranean dishes. This taverna provides an authentic dining experience with a touch of local charm.

Details:
Address: 45 Irish Town, Gibraltar GX11 1AA
Price Range: £15 - £30 per meal

Highlights:
Signature Dish: Paella, a flavorful rice dish cooked with an assortment of seafood, chicken, and vegetables, all seasoned with saffron and spices.
Warm Ambiance: The taverna's rustic interior creates a cozy and welcoming environment, perfect for a memorable meal.
Live Music: Enjoy occasional live music performances that add a cultural touch to your dining experience.

Fine Dining Restaurants

The Lounge Gastro Bar
The Lounge Gastro Bar is another excellent fine dining option in Gibraltar, known for its innovative dishes and chic ambiance. The restaurant offers a unique dining experience with a focus on modern European cuisine and expertly crafted cocktails.
Details:
Address: 10 Casemates Square, Gibraltar GX11 1AA
Price Range: £35 - £60 per meal
Highlights:
Creative Menu: Savor a selection of modern European dishes, each thoughtfully prepared with a blend of traditional and contemporary techniques.
Stylish Setting: Enjoy the trendy and stylish interior, perfect for a special night out or an elegant gathering.
Gourmet Cocktails: Complement your meal with one of their signature cocktails, expertly mixed to perfection.

Cafes and Bakeries

Cafes

Latte Café

Address: 21 Grand Casemates Square, Gibraltar GX11 1AA

Latte Café is a popular spot located in the bustling Grand Casemates Square. Known for its cozy atmosphere and friendly service, it offers a wide range of coffee drinks, teas, and light snacks. The café is a perfect place to relax and people-watch, with both indoor and outdoor seating available.

The Kasbar

Address: 5 Castle Street, Gibraltar GX11 1AA

The Kasbar is a vibrant and eclectic café situated in the historic area of Castle Street. It is well-loved for its healthy menu options, including a variety of vegetarian and vegan dishes. The colorful and quirky décor creates a unique and inviting atmosphere, making it a favorite among locals and tourists alike.

Piece of Cake Café

Address: 92 Irish Town, Gibraltar GX11 1AA

Piece of Cake Café is renowned for its homemade cakes and delightful afternoon teas. Located in the heart of Irish Town, this café offers a warm and welcoming atmosphere. It's a great place to enjoy a slice of cake, a cup of tea, and a chat with friends or family.

Costa Coffee

Address: ICC, Casemates Square, Gibraltar GX11 1AA

Costa Coffee, part of the well-known international chain, is located in the bustling Casemates Square. It offers a consistent selection of coffee, teas, and snacks, making it a reliable choice for a quick refreshment. The comfortable seating and familiar menu make it a popular spot for both locals and visitors.

Bakeries

Sacarello's Coffee Shop & Restaurant
Address: 57 Irish Town, Gibraltar GX11 1AA

Sacarello's is a historic coffee shop and restaurant known for its freshly baked bread, pastries, and a variety of delicious cakes. The warm and inviting atmosphere makes it a favorite spot for both locals and tourists.

Jury's Café & Wine Bar
Address: 275 Main Street, Gibraltar GX11 1AA

Jury's offers a delightful selection of baked goods, including pastries, cakes, and savory snacks. The café is also a great place to enjoy a glass of wine in a cozy and relaxed setting.

Panadería Gibraltar
Address: 34 Governors Parade, Gibraltar GX11 1AA

Panadería Gibraltar is a traditional bakery offering a variety of fresh bread, pastries, and cakes with a Mediterranean twist. It's an excellent place to pick up a quick snack or enjoy a leisurely coffee.

The Little Rock Café

Address: 12 Winston Churchill Avenue, Gibraltar GX11 1AA

The Little Rock Café is a family-run bakery known for its delicious cakes, pastries, and breakfast options. The friendly service and homey atmosphere make it a pleasant place to start your day.

Bake & Take

Address: Ocean Village Promenade, Gibraltar GX11 1AA

Bake & Take is a modern bakery with a wide selection of baked goods, from croissants and muffins to artisanal bread. Its convenient location and high-quality offerings make it a popular choice for both locals and visitors.

Local Markets and Food Tours

Gibraltar Market

Address: Fish Market Lane, Gibraltar GX11 1AA

The Gibraltar Market is a bustling hub where locals shop for fresh produce, meats, seafood, and a variety of other goods. It's a great place to experience the local culture and find fresh ingredients for a picnic or a home-cooked meal.

Highlights:

Fresh Produce: Browse stalls selling seasonal fruits and vegetables, sourced from local farms.

Seafood: Discover a wide selection of fresh fish and seafood, caught daily by local fishermen.
Local Delicacies: Sample traditional Gibraltarian foods and snacks, including freshly baked bread, pastries, and more.
Cultural Experience: Engage with friendly vendors and learn about the local culinary traditions and ingredients.

Local Food Tour with Gibraltar Food Tours
Address: Various locations around Gibraltar
Gibraltar Food Tours offers guided tours that take you through the best culinary spots in the city. These tours are designed to provide a comprehensive and enjoyable tasting experience, highlighting the diverse flavors of Gibraltar's cuisine.
Highlights:
Tasting Stops: Visit a variety of eateries, including traditional tavernas, modern cafes, and bakeries, sampling their signature dishes and treats.
Historical Insights: Learn about Gibraltar's rich history and cultural influences on its food from knowledgeable guides.
Local Favorites: Taste local specialties such as calentita, panissa, and rosto, and discover hidden culinary gems.
Interactive Experience: Enjoy an engaging and interactive experience, with opportunities to ask questions and learn from local chefs and food artisans.
Details:
Booking: Tours can be booked online or through local travel agencies. It's recommended to book in advance, especially during peak tourist seasons.
Duration: Tours typically last between 2 to 3 hours, covering several key culinary locations in Gibraltar.

Price Range: £40 - £70 per person, depending on the tour package and inclusions.

CHAPTER 9: Practical Information

Best Time to Visit

Gibraltar's unique location and climate make it a great destination to visit year-round. However, the best time to visit can depend on your personal preferences and the types of activities you want to enjoy. Here's a breakdown to help you decide when to plan your trip.

Spring (March to May)
Weather: Mild and pleasant, with average temperatures ranging from 15°C to 20°C (59°F to 68°F).
Highlights: Spring is a fantastic time for outdoor activities like hiking, bird watching, and exploring the Rock of Gibraltar. The Mediterranean Steps and other trails are particularly enjoyable in the cooler temperatures. The flora is also in full bloom, adding vibrant colors to the landscape.

Summer (June to August)
Weather: Warm to hot, with average temperatures ranging from 20°C to 30°C (68°F to 86°F).
Highlights: Summer is the peak tourist season, ideal for beach activities, water sports, and enjoying the long daylight hours. Events like Gibraltar Summer Nights, featuring live music and entertainment, make this a lively time to visit. However, it can be crowded, and accommodation prices may be higher.

Autumn (September to November)

Weather: Mild and gradually cooling, with temperatures ranging from 17°C to 25°C (63°F to 77°F).

Highlights: Autumn is another excellent time for outdoor activities and sightseeing. The weather is still warm, but with fewer crowds compared to summer. This is also a great time for cultural events, including Gibraltar National Day in September and the Gibraltar International Literary Festival in November.

Winter (December to February)

Weather: Mild and cooler, with temperatures ranging from 10°C to 17°C (50°F to 63°F).

Highlights: Winter is the off-peak season, making it a peaceful time to visit. It's perfect for exploring historical sites, museums, and enjoying local cuisine without the summer crowds. Christmas and New Year celebrations in Gibraltar are also festive and enjoyable.

Currency and Banking

Currency

Local Currency: The official currency of Gibraltar is the Gibraltar Pound (GIP), which is pegged at par with the British Pound Sterling (GBP). Gibraltar Pounds and British Pounds are used interchangeably.

Banknotes and Coins: Gibraltar issues its own banknotes and coins, which are similar in value and appearance to UK currency but feature unique designs specific to Gibraltar. UK currency is widely accepted, but Gibraltar currency is not typically accepted in the UK.

Exchange Rate: The exchange rate between the Gibraltar Pound and other currencies is the same as the British Pound. It's advisable to check current exchange rates before you travel.

Banking Services

ATMs: ATMs are widely available throughout Gibraltar, especially in popular tourist areas like Main Street and Casemates Square. Most ATMs accept international debit and credit cards.

Bank Branches: Major banks operating in Gibraltar include Barclays, NatWest, and the Gibraltar International Bank. These banks offer a range of services including currency exchange, cash withdrawals, and general banking services.

Opening Hours: Bank branches typically open from 9:00 AM to 4:30 PM, Monday to Friday. Some banks may have limited hours on Saturdays and are usually closed on Sundays and public holidays.

Currency Exchange

Where to Exchange: Currency can be exchanged at banks, exchange bureaus, and some hotels. Exchange rates and fees can vary, so it's wise to compare rates before making a transaction.

Credit and Debit Cards: Major credit and debit cards (Visa, MasterCard, American Express) are widely accepted in hotels, restaurants, and shops. However, it's a good idea to carry some cash for smaller establishments or markets.

Tips for Managing Money

Notify Your Bank: Before traveling, notify your bank of your trip to avoid any issues with card transactions.

Avoid Excessive Fees: Use ATMs associated with major banks to avoid excessive withdrawal fees. Check if your home bank has any partnerships with Gibraltar banks to minimize fees.

Carry a Mix of Payment Methods: Carry a mix of cash, credit cards, and debit cards to ensure you have multiple payment options.

Health and Safety

Health

Healthcare Services: Gibraltar has a well-established healthcare system, and the Gibraltar Health Authority (GHA) provides medical services similar to the UK's National Health Service (NHS). There are hospitals, clinics, and pharmacies available to address any health concerns.

Hospitals and Clinics: St. Bernard's Hospital is the main hospital in Gibraltar, offering a range of medical services including emergency care. There are also several clinics and private medical practices.

Address: St. Bernard's Hospital, Europort Road, Gibraltar GX11 1AA

Pharmacies: Pharmacies are widely available and typically open from 9:00 AM to 7:00 PM. Some may have extended hours or offer 24-hour service. They can provide over-the-counter medications and fill prescriptions.

Health Insurance: It's recommended to have comprehensive travel health insurance that covers medical expenses, including emergency evacuation. European Health Insurance Card (EHIC) holders are entitled to free or reduced-cost healthcare, but this is subject to change post-Brexit.

Vaccinations: No specific vaccinations are required for entry into Gibraltar, but it's always a good idea to ensure that your routine vaccinations are up to date.

Safety

General Safety: Gibraltar is considered a safe destination with low crime rates. However, it's always important to remain vigilant and take standard safety precautions.

Emergency Numbers:

Police, Fire, Ambulance: 112 or 199

Gibraltar Health Authority Emergency: +350 200 79700

Personal Safety Tips:

Stay Aware: Be mindful of your surroundings, especially in crowded tourist areas and at night.

Secure Valuables: Keep your belongings secure, use hotel safes, and avoid displaying valuables in public.

Local Laws: Familiarize yourself with local laws and customs. Gibraltar has strict laws against drug use and possession.

Travel Advisories: Check travel advisories from your home country's government for any updates or specific safety information related to Gibraltar.

Natural Hazards

Weather Conditions: Gibraltar enjoys a Mediterranean climate with mild winters and hot summers. Ensure you are prepared for the weather conditions during your visit. Use sunscreen, stay hydrated, and seek shade during the peak sun hours in summer.

Terrain: Gibraltar's terrain can be rugged, particularly in natural reserves and hiking areas. Wear appropriate footwear, stay on marked paths, and be cautious near cliff edges and steep drops.

Health and Safety Tips

Stay Hydrated: Drink plenty of water, especially during the hot summer months, to prevent dehydration.

Food Safety: Enjoy local cuisine, but ensure that food is well-cooked and fresh. Stick to bottled water if you're unsure about the tap water quality.

Emergency Contacts: Keep a list of emergency contacts, including the local embassy or consulate of your home country.

Travel Insurance: Always travel with comprehensive insurance that covers health, accidents, and unexpected travel disruptions.

Visa and Entry Requirements

Visa Requirements

European Union (EU) Citizens: Citizens of EU member states do not require a visa to enter Gibraltar for short stays. A valid passport or national identity card is sufficient.

United Kingdom (UK) Citizens: As Gibraltar is a British Overseas Territory, UK citizens do not require a visa to enter. A valid UK passport is sufficient.

Non-EU/Non-UK Citizens: Travelers from other countries may need a visa to enter Gibraltar. Visa requirements can vary, so it's essential to check with the nearest British Embassy or Consulate or consult the official Gibraltar government website for the most up-to-date information.

Entry Requirements

Passport Validity: Ensure your passport is valid for at least six months beyond your planned date of departure from Gibraltar.

Return/Onward Ticket: Travelers may be required to show proof of a return or onward ticket.

Sufficient Funds: You may need to demonstrate that you have sufficient funds to cover your stay in Gibraltar.

Customs and Immigration.

Entry Points: The main entry points to Gibraltar are via Gibraltar International Airport (GIB) and the land border with Spain at La Línea de la Concepción.

Customs Regulations: Gibraltar follows similar customs regulations to the UK. Be aware of restrictions on bringing certain goods, including high-value items, alcohol, tobacco, and food products.

Security Checks: Standard security checks apply at all entry points. Be prepared for bag inspections and personal searches if required.

Traveling from Spain

Land Border Crossing: If traveling from Spain, you can enter Gibraltar via the border at La Línea de la Concepción. Ensure you have the necessary documents, and be prepared for potential waiting times at the border, especially during peak hours.

Schengen Visa Holders: Travelers holding a valid Schengen visa can enter Gibraltar for short stays, provided their visa allows multiple entries and they have already entered the Schengen Area.

COVID-19 Entry Requirements

Health Measures: Due to the ongoing COVID-19 pandemic, additional health measures may be in place. This can include health declarations, proof of vaccination, negative COVID-19 test results, or quarantine requirements.

Official Guidance: Check the latest entry requirements related to COVID-19 on the official Gibraltar government website or through your airline before traveling.

Useful Contacts

Gibraltar Border and Coastguard Agency: For specific questions related to entry and visas, contact the Gibraltar Border and Coastguard Agency.

British Embassies and Consulates: If you need visa assistance, contact the nearest British Embassy or Consulate in your country.

Preparation Tips

Check Requirements: Always check the latest visa and entry requirements well in advance of your travel dates.

Carry Documentation: Carry all necessary travel documents, including your passport, visa (if required), travel itinerary, accommodation details, and proof of funds.

Stay Informed: Monitor travel advisories and updates from official sources to stay informed about any changes in entry requirements or health measures.

Local Customs and Laws

Local Customs

Language: English is the official language of Gibraltar, but many locals are bilingual and also speak Spanish. Learning a few basic phrases in Spanish can be appreciated.

Greeting Etiquette: A common greeting is a handshake. It's polite to greet people with a friendly "hello" or "good morning/afternoon."

Dress Code: Gibraltar is relatively relaxed about dress codes, but modesty is appreciated in religious sites and formal settings.

Tipping: Tipping is not mandatory but appreciated. A tip of 10-15% in restaurants and small tips for service staff such as taxi drivers and hotel porters are customary.

Public Behavior: Public displays of affection are generally acceptable, but excessive displays might be frowned upon. Respect public spaces and keep noise levels moderate.

Religious Practices

Religious Diversity: Gibraltar is home to various religious communities, including Christians, Muslims, Jews, and Hindus. Religious tolerance is an important value.

Places of Worship: Visitors are welcome to visit places of worship, but it's important to dress modestly and behave respectfully. Remove hats, cover shoulders, and avoid loud conversations inside these spaces.

Local Laws

Drug Laws: The possession, use, and trafficking of illegal drugs are strictly prohibited and punishable by law. This includes cannabis.

Alcohol Consumption: The legal drinking age in Gibraltar is 18. Drinking in public places is generally accepted, but it's best to consume alcohol responsibly and avoid public intoxication.

Smoking: Smoking is banned in enclosed public spaces, including bars, restaurants, and public transportation. Look for designated smoking areas.

Driving Laws:

Driving Side: In Gibraltar, you drive on the right-hand side of the road.

Seat Belts: Seat belts are mandatory for all passengers.

Mobile Phones: Using a mobile phone while driving is illegal unless you have a hands-free system.

Speed Limits: Adhere to posted speed limits, which are generally 50 km/h in urban areas and 80 km/h on highways.

Identification: Carry a form of identification with you at all times, such as a passport or a photocopy of your passport.

Respect for Wildlife: Gibraltar is home to the famous Barbary macaques. Do not feed or disturb them, as they are protected by law. Fines can be imposed for feeding the monkeys.

Public Safety

Emergency Numbers: The emergency number for police, fire, and ambulance services in Gibraltar is 112 or 199.

Harassment and Discrimination: Harassment and discrimination based on race, gender, religion, or sexual orientation are illegal and not tolerated.

Photography

Permission: Always ask for permission before taking photos of people, especially in private or sensitive situations.

Restricted Areas: Avoid taking photos in restricted areas, such as military installations or secure zones. Look for signs indicating photography restrictions.

Environmental Conservation

Littering: Littering is prohibited, and fines may be imposed. Use designated bins and recycling points.

Conservation Areas: Respect conservation areas and nature reserves. Stick to designated paths and avoid disturbing wildlife.

CHAPTER 10: Day Trips and Excursions

Tangier, Morocco
Just a short ferry ride across the Strait of Gibraltar, Tangier offers a vibrant mix of cultures, history, and architecture. It's a perfect destination for a day trip, providing a taste of North African charm.

Highlights:
Medina: Wander through the narrow streets of the old town, filled with markets, shops, and cafes.
Kasbah Museum: Explore this former palace, now a museum, showcasing the rich history and culture of Tangier.
Cave of Hercules: Visit this legendary cave with stunning views of the Atlantic Ocean.

Travel Details:
Ferry: Regular ferries run from Gibraltar or nearby Spanish ports to Tangier, with the journey taking about 1-2 hours.
Best Time to Visit: Spring and autumn for pleasant weather.

Tarifa, Spain

Tarifa, known for its strong winds and beautiful beaches, is a paradise for water sports enthusiasts, especially kitesurfers and windsurfers. It's also the southernmost point of mainland Europe.

Highlights:

Beaches: Relax on stunning beaches like Playa de Los Lances and Playa de Valdevaqueros.

Old Town: Stroll through the charming old town with its narrow streets, white-washed buildings, and lively atmosphere.

Castillo de Guzmán: Visit this historic castle offering panoramic views of the town and the Strait of Gibraltar.

Travel Details:

Distance: Approximately 45 minutes by car from Gibraltar.

Best Time to Visit: Summer for beach activities and water sports.

Algeciras, Spain
Algeciras is a major port city with a mix of industrial and cultural attractions. It's an excellent place to experience the local Spanish lifestyle and enjoy some great food.

Highlights:
Port Area: Explore the busy port and enjoy fresh seafood at local restaurants.
Plaza Alta: Visit the central square, surrounded by beautiful buildings and a vibrant market.
Parque María Cristina: Relax in this lovely park, perfect for a leisurely stroll or a picnic.

Travel Details:
Distance: About 30 minutes by car from Gibraltar.
Best Time to Visit: Year-round, as the climate is mild.

Estepona, Spain
Estepona is a picturesque town on the Costa del Sol, known for its beautiful beaches, charming old town, and vibrant cultural scene.
Highlights:
Old Town: Wander through the flower-lined streets of the historic center, filled with shops, cafes, and traditional Spanish architecture.

Beaches: Relax on pristine beaches like Playa de la Rada and Playa del Cristo.
Estepona Orchid House: Visit this unique botanical garden featuring a stunning collection of orchids.

Travel Details:
Distance: Approximately 1 hour by car from Gibraltar.
Best Time to Visit: Spring and summer for the best beach experience.

Marbella, Spain

Marbella is famous for its luxury lifestyle, upscale resorts, and vibrant nightlife. It's a fantastic destination for those looking to indulge in some glamour and relaxation.

Highlights:
Puerto Banús: Visit this luxurious marina, home to upscale shops, restaurants, and impressive yachts.
Old Town: Explore the charming old town with its narrow streets, historic buildings, and delightful plazas.
Beaches: Enjoy the sun on Marbella's golden beaches, such as Playa de la Fontanilla and Playa de Venus.

Travel Details:
Distance: About 1.5 hours by car from Gibraltar.
Best Time to Visit: Summer for beach activities and the lively atmosphere.

CHAPTER 11: Shopping and Souvenirs

Main Street Shopping
Main Street is Gibraltar's primary shopping area, offering a mix of high street brands, local shops, and duty-free stores. The pedestrian-friendly street is lined with historic buildings, making it a pleasant place to stroll and shop.

Highlights:
High Street Brands: Find popular British and international brands for clothing, accessories, and electronics.
Local Boutiques: Explore small, independent shops offering unique items and personalized service.
Jewelry and Watches: Discover a range of jewelers offering everything from luxury watches to unique handmade pieces.

Tips:
Look for sales and promotions, especially during the summer and post-Christmas sales.
Many shops close for a siesta in the afternoon, so plan your shopping trip accordingly.

Local Handicrafts

Gibraltar's local handicrafts make for unique and memorable souvenirs. These items reflect the cultural heritage and artistic skills of the local community.

Popular Handicrafts:
Lace and Embroidery: Handmade lace and embroidered linens are traditional crafts in Gibraltar, often found in local markets and specialty shops.
Ceramics: Beautifully crafted ceramics, including plates, bowls, and decorative tiles, showcase Mediterranean designs and colors.
Leather Goods: Quality leather products such as bags, belts, and wallets are popular buys, reflecting skilled craftsmanship.

Where to Buy:
Visit local markets, craft fairs, and boutique shops to find a variety of handmade items.

Duty-Free Shopping
Gibraltar is known for its duty-free shopping, offering significant savings on a wide range of products, including tobacco, alcohol, perfumes, and electronics.
Popular Duty-Free Items:
Tobacco and Cigarettes: Prices are significantly lower than in many other countries.
Alcohol: A wide selection of spirits, wines, and liqueurs at competitive prices.
Perfumes and Cosmetics: Major brands are available at reduced prices compared to mainland Europe.

Where to Buy:
Main Street and Casemates Square are popular areas for duty-free shopping.

Wines and Spirits
Gibraltar offers an excellent selection of wines and spirits, both local and international. These make for great souvenirs or gifts to take home.

Popular Choices:
Local Wines: Try wines from nearby Spanish regions such as Rioja, Ribera del Duero, and Andalusia.
Spirits: Gibraltar is known for its wide selection of gins, whiskeys, and other spirits, often available at duty-free prices.
Where to Buy:
Specialist wine and spirit shops on Main Street and surrounding areas.

Gibraltar Crystal

Gibraltar Crystal is a renowned local brand offering beautifully crafted crystal products. Each piece is handmade using traditional methods, making it a unique souvenir.

Popular Items:

Vases: Elegant and beautifully designed vases perfect for decorating your home.

Glassware: A range of glassware including wine glasses, tumblers, and decanters.

Ornaments: Delicate crystal ornaments and figurines, ideal as gifts or keepsakes.

Where to Buy:

Visit the Gibraltar Crystal showroom and factory at Grand Casemates Square to see the glassblowing process and purchase items directly.

CHAPTER 12: Itineraries

3-Day Itinerary

Day 1: Discover the Rock of Gibraltar
Morning: Take the cable car to the top of the Rock for panoramic views.
Midday: Explore St. Michael's Cave and the Great Siege Tunnels.
Afternoon: Visit the Apes' Den to see the famous Barbary macaques.
Evening: Stroll around Main Street for shopping and dinner.

Day 2: History and Heritage
Morning: Visit the Gibraltar Museum.
Midday: Tour the Moorish Castle.
Afternoon: Explore the City Under Siege Exhibition.
Evening: Dine at a local taverna and enjoy the vibrant nightlife.

Day 3: Coastal Delights
Morning: Relax at Catalan Bay.
Midday: Visit the Gibraltar Botanic Gardens (Alameda Gardens).
Afternoon: Take a Dolphin Watching Tour from the marina.
Evening: Enjoy a seafood dinner at a waterfront restaurant.

7-Day Itinerary

Day 1: The Essentials
Morning: Cable car ride to the top of the Rock of Gibraltar.
Midday: Visit St. Michael's Cave.
Afternoon: Explore the Apes' Den.
Evening: Dinner at Main Street.

Day 2: Historical Exploration
Morning: Visit the Gibraltar Museum.
Midday: Tour the Moorish Castle.
Afternoon: Explore the Great Siege Tunnels.
Evening: Relax with dinner at a local restaurant.

Day 3: Nature and Adventure
Morning: Hike the Mediterranean Steps.
Midday: Visit the Gibraltar Botanic Gardens.
Afternoon: Enjoy a Dolphin Watching Tour.
Evening: Dine at a waterfront restaurant.

Day 4: Day Trip to Tangier, Morocco
Morning: Ferry to Tangier.
Midday: Explore the Medina and Kasbah Museum.
Afternoon: Visit the Cave of Hercules.
Evening: Return to Gibraltar and relax.

Day 5: Cultural Day
Morning: Visit the City Under Siege Exhibition.
Midday: Explore the Shrine of Our Lady of Europe.
Afternoon: Visit the Trafalgar Cemetery.
Evening: Enjoy a cultural performance or event.

Day 6: Leisure and Relaxation
Morning: Spend time at Sandy Bay.
Midday: Lunch at a local café.
Afternoon: Visit local markets for shopping.
Evening: Indulge in a spa treatment.

Day 7: Final Explorations
Morning: Visit the Jews' Gate Cemetery.
Midday: Explore the Gibraltar Crystal Factory.
Afternoon: Final shopping on Main Street.
Evening: Farewell dinner at a fine dining restaurant.

Adventure Seeker's Itinerary

Day 1: Rock Climbing and Kayaking
Morning: Climb the Rock of Gibraltar's climbing routes.
Afternoon: Kayak around the coastline.
Evening: Dine at a local sports bar.

Day 2: Water Sports and Hiking
Morning: Paddleboard at Eastern Beach.
Afternoon: Scuba diving or snorkeling at Rosia Bay.
Evening: Enjoy a beachside barbecue.

Day 3: Hiking and Wildlife Watching
Morning: Hike the Mediterranean Steps.
Afternoon: Explore the Upper Rock Nature Reserve and visit Apes' Den.
Evening: Relax at a nature-themed café.

Day 4: Day Trip to Tarifa, Spain
Morning: Drive to Tarifa for kitesurfing or windsurfing.
Afternoon: Explore the old town and beaches.
Evening: Return to Gibraltar and unwind.

Family-Friendly Itinerary

Day 1: Fun and Education
Morning: Visit St. Michael's Cave.
Afternoon: Explore the Gibraltar Botanic Gardens.
Evening: Enjoy a family-friendly restaurant.

Day 2: Wildlife and Nature
Morning: See the Barbary macaques at Apes' Den.
Afternoon: Visit the Alameda Wildlife Conservation Park.
Evening: Take a family walk around Main Street.

Day 3: Beach Day
Morning: Spend the day at Catalan Bay.
Afternoon: Build sandcastles and enjoy water activities.
Evening: Have a casual dinner at a beachfront café.

Day 4: Dolphin Watching
Morning: Dolphin watching tour from the marina.
Afternoon: Lunch at a marina restaurant.
Evening: Visit the Great Siege Tunnels.

Cultural Explorer's Itinerary

Day 1: Historical Sites
Morning: Visit the Gibraltar Museum.
Afternoon: Tour the Moorish Castle and City Under Siege Exhibition.
Evening: Dinner at a traditional taverna.

Day 2: Religious and Cultural Sites
Morning: Visit the Shrine of Our Lady of Europe.
Afternoon: Explore the Trafalgar Cemetery and Jews' Gate Cemetery.
Evening: Enjoy a cultural performance.

Day 3: Local Experiences
Morning: Explore Main Street and local markets.
Afternoon: Visit Gibraltar Crystal Factory and learn about glassmaking.
Evening: Dinner at a fine dining restaurant with local cuisine.

Day 4: Day Trip to Algeciras, Spain
Morning: Drive to Algeciras and visit the port area.
Afternoon: Explore Plaza Alta and Parque María Cristina.
Evening: Return to Gibraltar and relax.

CONCLUSION

As we conclude this Gibraltar Travel Guide 2024, we hope you are now equipped with all the knowledge and inspiration you need to make the most of your visit to this remarkable destination. Gibraltar, with its rich history, stunning landscapes, and unique blend of cultures, offers an unforgettable experience for every traveler.

From exploring the heights of the Rock of Gibraltar and mingling with the Barbary macaques to delving into the fascinating history of the Great Siege Tunnels and enjoying the vibrant culinary scene, there is something here for everyone. Whether you're an adventure seeker, a cultural explorer, or a family looking for a fun and educational holiday, Gibraltar has it all.

Remember to take advantage of the practical tips and itineraries provided in this guide to plan your days efficiently and ensure you don't miss out on any of the highlights. The best time to visit, currency and banking information, health and safety tips, and local customs and laws will help you navigate Gibraltar smoothly and respectfully.

Embrace the spirit of adventure as you embark on day trips to nearby destinations like Tangier, Tarifa, Algeciras, Estepona, and Marbella. Each place adds a different flavor to your journey, enriching your travel experience.

As you shop for unique souvenirs, savor the local cuisine, and enjoy the warm hospitality of Gibraltar's residents, you'll create memories that will last a lifetime. From the bustling streets of Main Street to the serene beaches and nature reserves, every moment in Gibraltar offers a new opportunity for discovery and delight.

We wish you a safe, enjoyable, and unforgettable trip to Gibraltar. May your journey be filled with wonderful experiences, new friendships, and a deeper appreciation for the beauty and diversity of this extraordinary destination. Happy travels!

No 2 Bus to Europa Point
Cable Car to the Top of the Rock Veiws Brilliant.
Best time to visit early spring, winter.
7/9/25 - 14/9/25 with Cambrian Crew + Two wives Marie and Lorrine (Bit by a monkey)
Indian Restaurant in the Marina (Good).
Italian Restaurant PAPA RAZZI. Cornwall lane. Not Good.

Holiday Inn Express. ON. Nice People.
- Language Buds?
Self Catering Accom. Catelan Bay?
For Winter Breaks.

Rosia Bay
Europa Point ✓
Main Street ✓

Gibralta is crossley over populated, traffic is Horrendus, All the New Build is Not in Reach of the Local People, if they dont stop Building there will be problems ahead.
The traffic will lead to Air Quality Problems
The people like their independance But Rely on UK for Safety. I find Most of them UnFriendly or ignorant. (my opinion) The Spanish do all the cleaning in the hotels.

If me was to come here again get a hotel in the centre (Quick Break) Try Self Catering Catalan Bay)

Gibraltons speak a mixture of Tongues English Spanish a Llaniti.